QUILLING
for beginners

QUILLING
for beginners

Jean Woolston-Hamey

KANGAROO PRESS

This book is dedicated to the five wonderful children who worked hard to test these patterns: Jacob, Sharai, Martiiqua, Sharmonee and Travis. Thank you, kids.

QUILLING FOR BEGINNERS
First published in Australia in 2004 by Kangaroo Press
an imprint of Simon & Schuster (Australia) Pty Ltd
20 Barcoo Street, East Roseville NSW 2069

A Viacom Company
Sydney New York London Toronto Singapore

Visit our website at www.simonsaysaustralia.com.au

National Library of Australia
Cataloguing-in-Publication data

  Woolston-Hamey Jean.
  Quilling : for beginners.

  ISBN 0 7318 1231 X

Paper quillwork. I. Title.

745.54

Cover and internal design by Anna Warren, Warren Ventures Pty Ltd
Typeset in Bembo 12/16pt
Photography by PhotoFX
Printed in China through Colorcraft Ltd., Hong Kong

10 9 8 7 6 5 4 3 2 1

CONTENTS

INTRODUCTION

When I first went looking for a quilling book, back in 1992, there was nothing especially for beginners – nothing to take me through the steps of the simplest shapes or to explain the little hints that make quilling easier. Since that time, I have had many people – adults, children, even primary school teachers – looking for a simple and inexpensive craft to learn and teach. Again, there was nothing just for beginners. I spent considerable time teaching the basics of quilling and helping people of all ages to get started. Although what I most enjoy is creating more elaborate patterns, the overwhelming need for a beginners' book has been so strong that I felt I had to do something to fill this gap. Many books give you the basic shapes but none gives you graded patterns to develop your skills simply and easily, as this book does.

On pages 44–8 is the Children's Gallery. These pieces were done by five keen children, two boys and three girls, aged from six to 12.

I hope you find this book helpful in beginning your quilling craft. Once you master these patterns, you should have very little trouble taking on much bigger and more challenging pieces from almost any quilling book. Good luck, and enjoy.

QUILLING BASICS

This book was created to help you develop the simple skills to make wonderful quilling. Basically there are just three shapes to learn. These shapes fit together in different ways to create lovely or interesting designs and patterns.

If a design appears too complex, just look at the simple shapes that comprise it: how many tight or loose coil shapes and so on. Once you break patterns down in this way, almost all designs become simple. Don't be afraid to create your own designs. Let your imagination carry you away. Quilling is fun, creative and inexpensive.

NOTE: It is very important to read all instructions carefully; don't just follow the photographs.

ATTRACTIVE QUILLED DESIGNS CREATED FROM COILS, SCROLLS, TEARDROPS AND FRINGING

TOOLS

Types of tools used in quilling

There are different types of **quilling tools**. But to begin with, it is best to learn with a **needle eye tool** (a sewing needle with the eye opened to form a prong, set in a wooden handle). This is the tool that I use. Avoid aluminium tools; they will make your fingers black and your work dirty. A **round pin tool** (a tiny metal tube with a side slit) is good for pieces that require a round centre hole and wide strips. **Needle point tools** come later if you wish. You will need **small sharp scissors** for fringing and for cutting ends. **Tweezers** prevent your fingers from becoming sticky. Use a **toothpick** to apply tiny amounts of glue. You will need a **measuring rule**; a small plastic one is fine. Use a **tiny bulldog clip** as a depth gauge for fringing. **Cotton buds** can be used to remove excess glue. A **damp cloth** will keep fingers and tools clean.

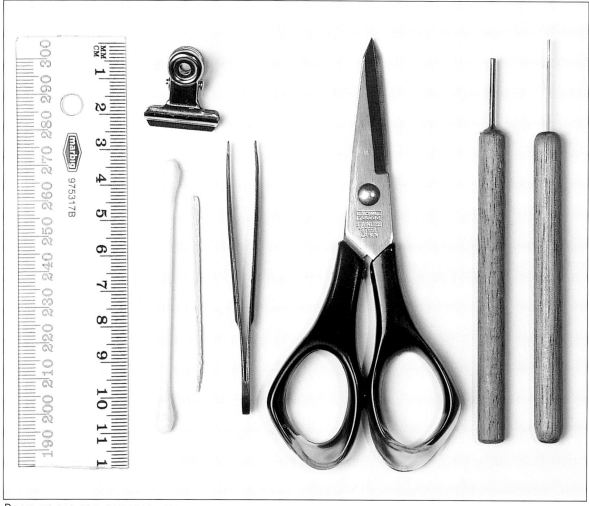

BASIC TOOLS FOR QUILLING: SMALL PLASTIC MEASURING RULE, TINY BULLDOG CLIP, COTTON BUD, TOOTHPICK, TWEEZERS, SMALL SHARP SCISSORS, ROUND PIN TOOL AND NEEDLE EYE TOOL

PAPER

What types of paper can be quilled?

Most paper can be quilled, but some types are better than others.

What types of paper are available?

Paper is graded by weight, in grams per square metre, or gsm. This denotes the thickness of the paper.

1. The very best **quilling paper** is 160 gsm and is rather expensive for beginners. It has cloth fibres added to help it hold its colour for a long time. This paper is usually sold in packets of cut strips in a range of colours and sizes, or in large sheets of one colour that need to be cut to size. Wait until you become really proficient, then make lasting pieces from this paper.

2. **Letter writing paper** is very good for quilling. It is usually sold in pads of one colour. The colours are generally soft shades and the weight varies from 80 to 120 gsm. Buy cheaper pads – they quill just as well as expensive ones. Pads of writing paper will need to be cut to size.

3. **Photocopy paper** works well for all quillers. It comes in a wide range of colours, is 80 gsm, cheap and easy to use. Office supply shops often sell single A4 sheets of this paper or stock it in pads of assorted colours. Again, it will need to be cut to size.

   I started quilling with photocopy paper and still use it to test patterns before using the more expensive papers. There is now a full colour range of 80 gsm cut strip papers available from many craft shops.

4. **Gift wrapping paper** is fun to use, but keep in mind that the colour or pattern is printed on one side only. However, you can achieve many interesting effects using this difference. These papers are usually 60 to 80 gsm, which is fine for quilling. Once again, they will need cutting.

5. **Construction pads** are not expensive and are very useful for quilling and making gift cards. Some pads have papers of different thicknesses, ranging from 70 to 160 gsm, and come in repeat colours. Others have repeat-colour sheets that are all 80 gsm. These pads are often available at supermarkets and newsagencies. But once again, they will need to be cut to size.

6. **Handmade papers** can be used, but unless you are making the paper yourself, it could be expensive. Be careful of the type you use; sometimes the fibres in such papers are rather small, meaning that the paper could crack when quilled.

Handmade papers can make beautiful quilling using special colours and textures.

What papers are not suited to quilling?

Airmail paper, tissue and cellophane are all too soft. Toilet paper is best left in the bathroom.

How wide should the paper strips be?

The width for most quilling is around 3 mm (⅛ inch). This is the best size to learn with. Another good size is 6 mm (¼ inch). The 1.5-mm (1/16-inch) strips make very fine-looking, delicate pieces. There are wider strips available for fringing work and candle making.

Pre-cut papers

These are available in packets of 100 strips in widths of 1.5 mm (1/16 inch), 3 mm (⅛ inch), 6 mm (¼ inch) and 9 mm (⅜ inch). A large colour range is available, both in one-colour packs and packs of mixed colours. Pre-cut papers are recommended if you want to spend your time quilling, not cutting paper.

Cut or tear?

Many patterns require long or pre-cut strips to be cut or torn into shorter lengths before they are made into shapes. Whether you cut or tear a strip depends on what is to be done with it.

TIPS

1. If the end is to be glued − tear it.
2. If the end will not be glued − cut it.

Glue

Use white PVA or white craft glue. Both of these glues dry clear and can be cleaned up with water. The secret of good quilling is to use as little glue as possible.

TIP

Smear only a tiny drop of glue when sticking strips together.

SHAPES

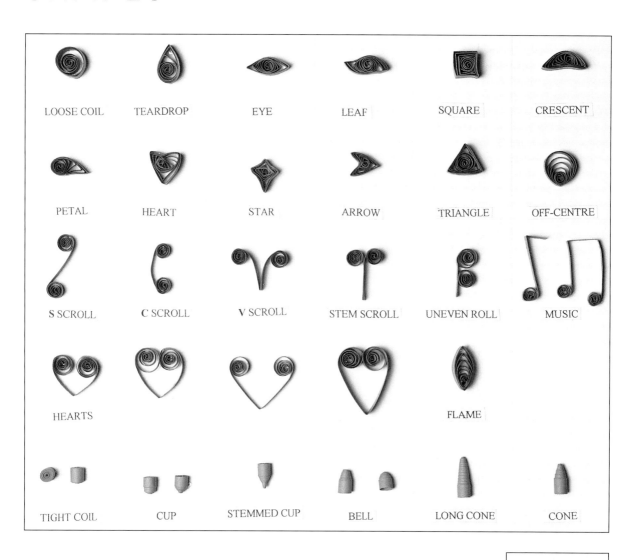

LOOSE COIL TEARDROP EYE LEAF SQUARE CRESCENT

PETAL HEART STAR ARROW TRIANGLE OFF-CENTRE

S SCROLL C SCROLL V SCROLL STEM SCROLL UNEVEN ROLL MUSIC

HEARTS FLAME

TIGHT COIL CUP STEMMED CUP BELL LONG CONE CONE

The following are the six basic quilling shapes. You should learn these first.

| Tight coil | Eye | Teardrop |
| Loose coil | S scroll | C scroll |

Other shapes you will need to make for these projects are:

Leaf	Crescent	Heart
Cone	Cup	Dome
Fringed tight coil	Daisy	

DAISY

FRINGED TIGHT COIL

Once you have mastered the tension control, you will be able to create all the patterns on the following pages. Keep your first attempts to see how you improve as you go along. All patterns are glued onto light card 9 cm (3 ½ inches) long and 5 cm (2 inches) wide. Heavy paper can also be used; this can be used flat or folded into a small card that opens up.

Using the needle eye quilling tool

Your first project is Confetti Border, made with tight coils of different colours. This will help you to develop correct tension: too tight, and the centre will pull out when you try to take it off the tool; too loose, and it will not hold the shape, and will slip around the tool and fall off. If your tension is not correct, just start again. All patterns can be made using any of the tools mentioned. The size of the finished shape will vary according to the size of the centre hole, which in turn depends on which tool is used.

TIGHT COIL patterns 1 & 2

Hold the tool in one hand. With the other hand, hold one end of the paper between thumb and index finger. The loose section of the paper strip should sit over the space made by the finger and thumb. Now push about 3 mm (⅛ inch) of the tip of the paper into the space at the top of the tool. Gently make one full turn of the tool to lock the end of the paper behind itself.

It doesn't matter whether you go clockwise or anti-clockwise; go whichever way feels most comfortable. Continue to turn the tool in the same direction, allowing the paper to feed through your thumb and finger (this is known as finger tension control). When you approach the end of the paper, do not continue to coil as this will increase the tension on the tool and make the coil too tight to remove.

Now you need to glue the end. Turn the tool until the end of the paper is facing towards you. Now, using your index finger only, apply enough pressure from behind the coil to stop the paper from unwinding. Allow the thumb and the

other fingers to hold the handle of the tool. This will allow you to use your other hand to apply a tiny bit of glue to the loose end and stick the loose end to the side of the coil. Allow the glue to dry before letting go, then gently push up from under the coil against the needle shaft to remove the shape from the tool.

TIP

Never pull your work upward to get it off the tool – always push it up from below.

LOOSE COIL pattern 3

Make a tight coil, but do not glue the end. Turn the tool upside down and allow the coil to fall off the tool and unwind a little. It will stop unwinding by itself; when it does, glue the loose end. The tighter a tight coil is wound, the less unwinding it will do, so when making a loose coil, coil the paper just a little more loosely than you normally would.

TIP

Remember that the tighter you coil, the smaller the loose coil will be.

For even loose coils, you will need even tension; otherwise your coils will vary in diameter. At craft shops you can purchase boards with holes to place the coils in before gluing them, to ensure that the coil sizes remain exact.

PATTERNS

CONFETTI BORDER

Paper 80 gsm, 3 mm (⅛ inch) wide

Colour Nine different bright colours

Quilling shape Tight coil

Construction

Cut 27 strips, each 3 mm (⅛) wide by 6 cm (2 ⁵⁄₁₆ inches) long, in the colours of your choice.

Some of the strips will have one torn end and one cut end. Coil from the cut end and glue the torn end. Form each strip into a tight coil.

TIP

If any of your coils, or 'tiny posts', have 'tiny noses' – that is, slightly conical ends – use the handle end of your tool to apply gentle pressure on top of the coils. This will give them flat tops and bottoms.

Mounting

First, arrange all the pieces on the card without using glue. Position two rows along the top of the card and two rows down one side, arranging the colours to your satisfaction. When you are happy with your layout, glue the pieces down, one at a time. Use a toothpick to apply a very small amount of glue to the bottom of each 'tiny post' and affix it to the card.

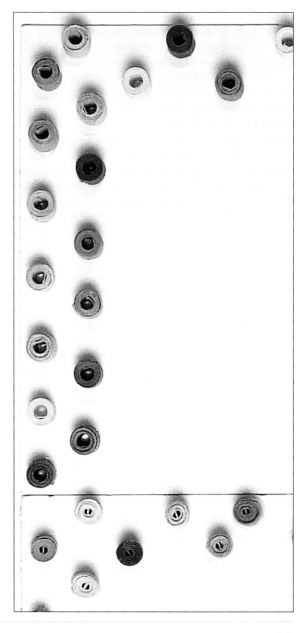

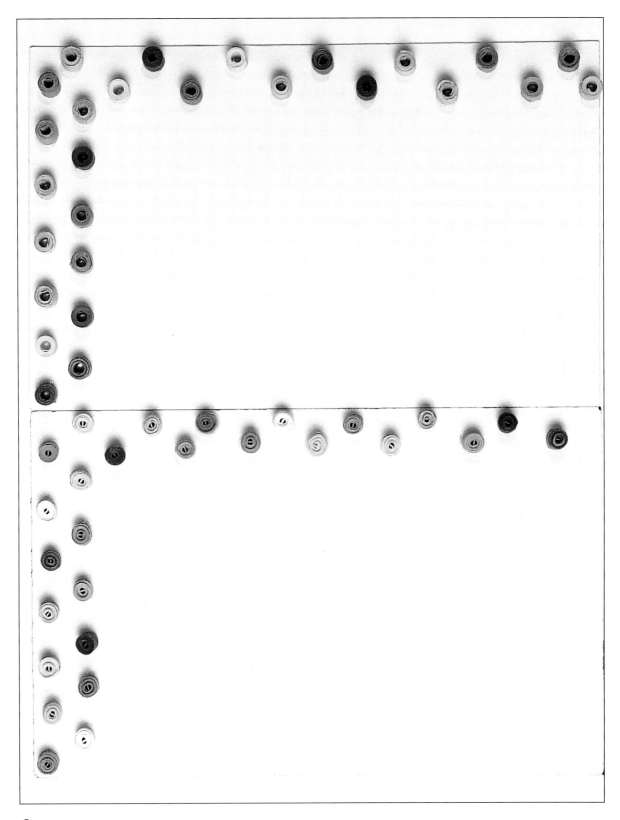

Confetti border

RISING BUBBLES

Paper 80 gsm, 3 mm (⅛ inch) wide

Colour One colour

Quilling shape Tight coil

Construction

Cut six strips, as follows:

- One strip, 3 mm (⅛ inch) by 20 cm (8 inches)
- One strip, 3 mm (⅛ inch) by 15 cm (6 inches)
- One strip, 3 mm (⅛ inch) by 10 cm (4 inches)
- One strip, 3 mm (⅛ inch) by 6 cm (2 ⁵⁄₁₆ inches)
- One strip, 3 mm (⅛ inch) by 4 cm (1 ½ inches)
- One strip, 3 mm (⅛ inch) by 2 cm (¾ inch)

Form each strip into a tight coil. Remember to coil each strip from the cut end. If necessary, use the end of your tool to ensure that the finished coils have flat tops, as described on page 15.

Mounting

First, arrange all the pieces on the card without using glue. At the bottom left-hand edge of the card, position the largest 'bubble'. Spacing them evenly, place the remaining bubbles along the left edge in descending order of size, finishing at the top with the smallest bubble. When you are happy with your layout, glue the pieces down, one at a time.

BALLOONS

Paper 80 gsm, 3 mm (⅛ inch) wide

Colour Four colours: use three colours for three of the balloons and one colour for the fourth balloon and the strings

Quilling shape Loose coil

Construction

For the balloons, cut four strips (one from each colour), each 3 mm (⅛ inch) by 20 cm (8 inches). Coil, then allow to unroll to about 12 mm (½ inch) in diameter. Glue the torn end and allow to dry.

For the strings, cut four strips of the same colour, each 3 mm (⅛ inch) by 3 cm (1 ¼ inches). Apply glue to 6 mm (¼ inch) of one end of one strip. Lay another strip on top, glue as before, then lay a third strip on top, so that you have three strips glued together at one end. Spread the tops of the strings apart.

For the runaway balloon string, take the remaining strip and bend it into a wavy shape.

MOUNTING

First, arrange all the pieces on the card without using glue. When you are happy with the layout, glue the pieces down, one at a time. Attach the three-string piece by gluing along the edge of the strips; position it at the bottom edge of the card. Now attach one balloon to the end of each string. Position the runaway balloon, then glue along the edge of the wavy string and fix it in place.

DEW DROPS

Paper 80 gsm, 3 mm (⅛ inch) wide

Colour Two colours: one for the droplets, one for the blades of grass

Quilling shapes Loose coil, teardrop

Construction

For the dew drops, cut:

- Seven strips, each 3 mm (⅛ inch) by 4 cm (1 ½ inches). Form each strip into a loose coil about 3 mm (⅛ inch) in diameter and glue the ends.
- One strip, 3 mm (⅛ inch) by 6 cm (2 ⁵⁄₁₆ inches). Form into a loose coil about 6 mm (¼ inch) in diameter and glue the end.

When the glue is dry, gently squeeze part of the coil (usually near the glue join) to form a pointed end. This gives you the teardrop shape.

For the blades of grass, cut:

- One strip, 3 mm (⅛ inch) by 7 cm (2 ¾ inches). Bend this strip 5 cm (2 inches) from one end.
- One strip, 3 mm (⅛ inch) by 4.5 cm (1 ¾ inches). Bend this strip 3 cm (1 ¼ inches) from one end.
- One strip, 3 mm (⅛ inch) by 3 cm (1 ¼ inches). Curve this strip gently to form one blade of grass.
- One strip, 3 mm (⅛ inch) by 2 cm (¾ inch). Curve this strip gently to form the other blade of grass.

MOUNTING

First, arrange all the pieces on the card without using glue. When you are happy with the layout, glue the pieces down, one at a time. First glue the blades of grass on edge.

Then glue the dew drops along the upper side of the bent part of each grass blade. Suspend the teardrop shape by its point at the tip of the smaller bent grass blade.

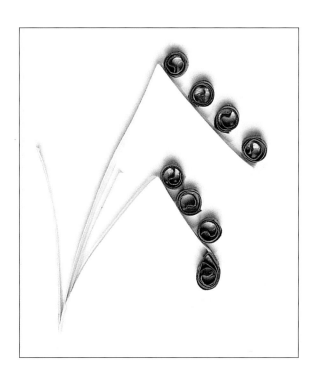

TEARDROP BORDER

Paper 80 gsm, 3 mm (⅛ inch) wide

Colours Two colours: one for the teardrops, one for the tight coils

Quilling shapes Teardrop, tight coil

Construction

For the teardrops, cut 12 strips, each 3 mm (⅛ inch) by 10 cm (4 inches).

Form each strip into a loose coil 6 mm (¼ inch) in diameter. Press one end of each loose coil to form a teardrop shape, as described in the previous project.

For the tight coils, cut 12 strips, each 3 mm (⅛ inch) by 5 cm (2 inches). Form each strip into a tight coil.

MOUNTING

First, arrange all the pieces on the card without glue. When you are happy with the layout, glue the pieces down, one at a time. Glue the centres first, then glue the teardrops at an angle.

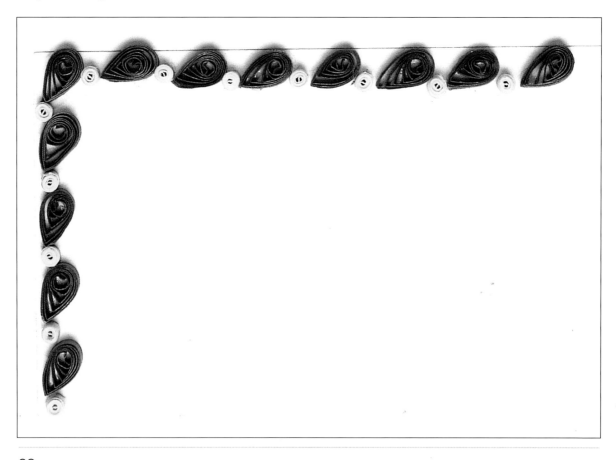

FLOWER SPRAY

Paper 80 gsm, 3 mm (⅛ inch) wide

Colour Two or four colours: one colour for the leaves, one colour (or three shades of one colour) for the blossoms

Quilling shapes Tight coil, eye

Construction

For the blossoms, cut:

- Six strips, each 3 mm (⅛ inch) by 10 cm (4 inches). Form into tight coils.
- Six strips, each 3 mm (⅛ inch) by 6 cm (2 ⁵⁄₁₆ inches). Form into tight coils.
- Three strips, each 3 mm (⅛ inch) by 2 cm (¾ inch). Form into tight coils.

For the leaves, cut 4 strips, each 3 mm (⅛ inch) by 10 cm (4 inches). Form each into an eye shape by making loose coils 6 mm (¼ inch) in diameter then pressing each coil into a point on both sides.

For the stem, cut one strip, 3 mm (⅛ inch) by 4.5 cm (1 ¾ inches). Gently curve to form the stem.

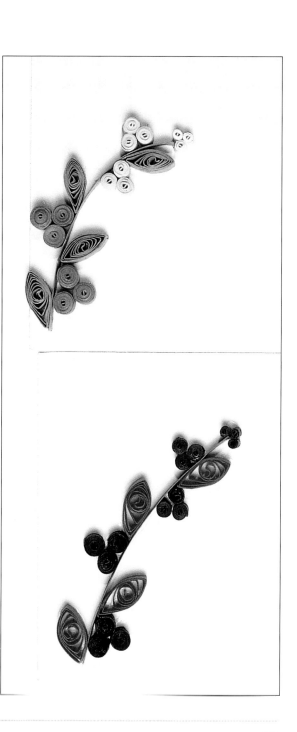

Mounting

First, arrange all the pieces on the card without glue. Position the stem on its edge, starting at the bottom corner of the card. Add the larger of the blossoms in two groups of three, one group on either side of the stem, starting towards the bottom. Place the medium blossoms in two groups of three further up the stem and finally the three small blossoms at the very tip. Position the leaves as shown in the photograph. When you are happy with the layout, glue the pieces down, one at a time.

SIMPLE DRAGONFLY

Paper 80 gsm, 3 mm (⅛ inch) wide

Colour Two colours: one for the head and body, one for the wings

Quilling shapes Tight coil, eye

Construction

For the head and body, cut:

- 1 strip, 3 mm (⅛ inch) by 30 cm (12 inches). Form into a tight coil. This piece will form the head.
- 1 strip, 3 mm (⅛ inch) by 20 cm (8 inches). Form into a tight coil.
- 1 strip, 3 mm (⅛ inch) by 15 cm (6 inches). Form into a tight coil.
- 1 strip, 3 mm (⅛ inch) by 10 cm (4 inches). Form into a tight coil.
- 1 strip, 3 mm (⅛ inch) by 7 cm (2 ¾ inches). Form into a tight coil.
- 1 strip, 3 mm (⅛ inch) by 5 cm (2 inches). Form into a tight coil.
- 1 strip, 3 mm (⅛ inch) by 3 cm (1 ¼ inches). Form into a tight coil.
- 1 strip, 3 mm (⅛ inch) by 1.5 cm (⅝ inch). Form into a tight coil.

All of the above pieces will form the body.

- 1 strip, 3 mm (⅛ inch) by 1 cm (⁷⁄₁₆ inch). Form into a tight coil. This piece will form the tail.

For the wings, cut:

- Two strips, each 3 mm (⅛ inch) by 30 cm (12 inches). Form into a loose coil 1.5 cm (⅝ inch) in diameter then press each end of the coil to make an eye shape.
- Two strips, each 3 mm (⅛ inch) by 10 inches (25 cm). Form into a loose coil of 1 cm (⁷⁄₁₆ inch) diameter then press each end of the coil to make an eye shape.

MOUNTING

First, arrange all the pieces on the card without glue. When you are happy with the layout, glue the pieces down, one at a time. Position the head coil and all the body coils (but not the tail coil) flat, as for the Rising Bubbles project on page 17, but touching each other. They can be arranged in either a straight or a curved line. Remember to leave enough space at the edges of the card for the wings. The tail coil is glued on its side at the very end of the body. Now position the wings between the head coil and the first of the body coils, putting the largest wing closest to the head on each side and the smaller wing below.

Box decorated with the simple dragonfly shape, using tight coils, eye shapes and S scrolls

THREE-PETAL FLOWER AND BUD

Paper 80 gsm, 3 mm (⅛ inch) wide

Colour Four colours: one for the outsides of the petals, one for the flower centre and the insides of the petals, one for the bud, one for the leaves and stem

Quilling shapes Tight coil, teardrop (using two colours), eye

Construction

For the flower centre, cut one strip, 3 mm (⅛ inch) by 5 cm (2 inches). Form into a tight coil.

For the bud centre, cut one strip, 3 mm (⅛ inch) by 3 cm (1 ¼ inches). Form into a tight coil.

Each of the petals is formed from two colours. For the insides of the petals, cut three strips, each 3 mm (⅛ inch) by 5 cm (2 inches), from one colour.

For the outside of the petal, cut three strips, each 3 mm (⅛ inch) by 3 cm (1 ¼ inches), from another colour. Take one strip of each colour and join at one end to form one long strip. Repeat with the remaining strips so that you have three longer strips. Coil from the inside colour end to form a loose coil of 6 mm (¼ inch), then press at each end to make an eye shape.

For the bud, cut three strips, each 3 mm (⅛ inch) by 3 cm (1 ¼ inches). Form each strip into a tight coil.

For the larger leaves, cut three strips, each 3 mm (⅛ inch) by 8 cm (3 ⅛ inches). Form into a loose coil 6 mm (¼ inch), then press at each end to form an eye shape.

For the smaller leaf, cut one strip, 3 mm (⅛ inch) by 4 cm (1 ½ inches). Form into a loose coil 3 mm (⅛ inch), then press at each side to form an eye shape.

For the long stem, cut one strip, 3 mm (⅛ inch) by 3 cm (1 ¼ inches) and curve slightly in opposite directions at each end. This piece will be attached on its edge.

For the short stem, cut one strip, 3 mm (⅛ inch) by 2 cm (¾ inch) and curve it slightly in opposite directions at each end. This piece will be attached on its edge.

Mounting

First, arrange all the pieces on the card without glue. When you are happy with the layout, glue the pieces down, one at a time. Start with the stems, then add the flower and buds, then the leaves.

VINE OF FLOWERS AND LEAVES

Paper 80 gsm, 3 mm (⅛ inch) wide

Colour Three colours: one for the petals, one for the centres, one for the leaves and stem

Quilling shapes Tight coil, teardrop, eye

Construction

For the stem, cut one strip, 3 mm (⅛ inch) by 4.5cm (1 ¾ inches). Curve this piece into a wavy line.

For the petals, cut twelve strips, each 3 mm (⅛ inch) by 5 cm (2 inches). Form each strip into a loose coil to a diameter of 3 mm (⅛ inch), then press at one end to form a teardrop.

For the centres, cut four strips, each 3 mm (⅛ inch) by 2 cm (¾ inch). Form each strip into a tight coil.

For the leaves, cut seven strips, each 3 mm (⅛ inch) by 5 cm (2 inches). Form each strip into a loose coil 3 mm (⅛ inch) in diameter, then press at both ends to form an eye.

MOUNTING

First, arrange all the pieces on the card without glue. When you are happy with the layout, glue the pieces down, one at a time, in the following order. First, glue the stem on its edge and position on the card.

Next, position the centres against the curve of the stem; they can be placed all on one side or divided between both sides.

Next, add the petals, using three for each centre, placing them in a fan shape with the pointed ends facing inwards and touching each other.

Each leaf is attached by one point to the stem, as shown in the photograph.

NOTE When done all in white, this pattern is very pretty for wedding cards.

CORNER HEARTS

Paper 80 gsm, 3 mm (⅛ inch) wide

Colour One or more colours

Quilling shapes Hearts (one open, six closed), C scroll folded in half

Construction

Cut six strips, each 3 mm (⅛ inch) by 8 cm (3 ⅛ inches). Fold each strip in half and coil it down to the centre fold. Remove the tool, coil the other side, and remove the tool. Allow the piece to unwind. Now unroll each coil for about 1 cm (⁷⁄₁₆ inch) and glue the coils together where they touch at the top.

Cut one strip, 3 mm (⅛ inch) by 8 cm (3 ⅛ inches). Repeat as for the other hearts, but do not glue the coils together.

First, arrange all the pieces on the card without glue. Position the closed hearts first, placing them with their points toward three of the corners of the card. In the top left-hand corner, position the three closed hearts and the remaining open heart with their points touching. When you are happy with the layout, glue the pieces down, one at a time.

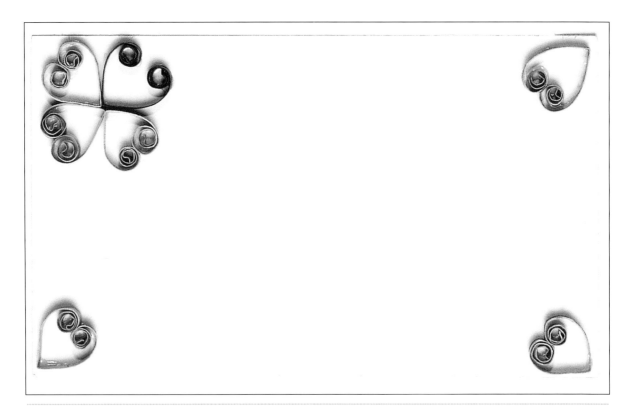

SCROLL BORDER

Paper 80 gsm, 3 mm (⅛ inch) wide

Colour Two colours

Quilling shapes Tight coil, teardrop, C scroll

TIP

To keep scroll coils in place, put a tiny spot of glue where the coil touches the straight part of the strip.

Construction

Cut:

- Eleven strips, each 3 mm (⅛ inch) by 5 cm (2 inches). Form each strip into a C scroll by coiling from both ends on the same side, leaving a 1 cm (⁷⁄₁₆ inch) straight section in the centre.
- Seven strips, each 3 mm (⅛ inch) by 5 cm (2 inches). Form each strip into a tight coil.
- Four strips, each 3 mm (⅛ inch) by 8 cm (3 ⅛ inches). Form each strip into a loose coil to a diameter of 6 mm (¼ inch) and press one side to form a teardrop shape.

Mounting

First, arrange all the pieces on the card without glue. Position three of the tight coils at the corners and another tight coil in the centre of the long side. Then position the corner and centre C scrolls as shown in the photograph. Now fill in the design with the other C scrolls, reversing the centre coil position on the short side. Position the remaining three tight coils: place one inside the scroll on the short side and one in each of the spaces between the scrolls on the long side. Now add the teardrops, placing their points against the centre of the scrolls as shown in the photograph. When you are happy with the layout, glue the pieces down, one at a time.

NOTE This is a good pattern for men's or boys' cards.

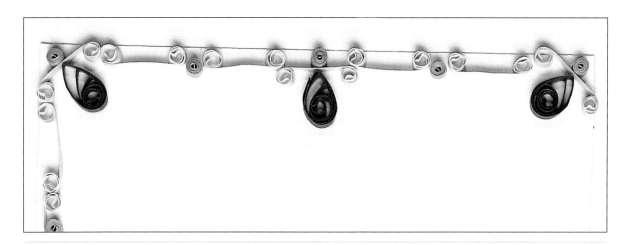

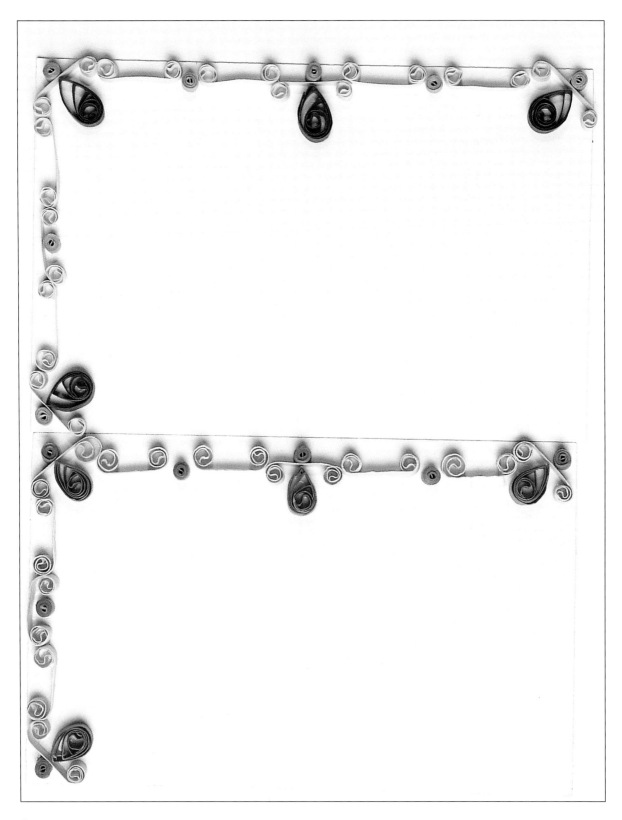

SCROLL BORDER

THREE-PETAL FLOWER WITH SCROLLS

Paper 80 gsm, 3 mm (⅛ inch) wide

Colour Two colours

Quilling shapes Teardrop, tight coil, S scroll

TIP

To keep scroll coils in place, put a tiny spot of glue where the coil touches the straight part of the strip.

Construction

Cut:

- Eight strips, each 3 mm (⅛ inch) by 5 cm (2 inches). Form each strip into an S scroll by coiling from one end, then turning the strip over and coiling from the other end. Leave a 1 cm (⁷⁄₁₆ inch) straight section in the centre just as you do with the C scroll shape. The finished S scroll should be 12 mm (⅝ inch) long.

- Three strips, each 3 mm (⅛ inch) by 10 cm (4 inches). Form each strip into a loose coil to 6 mm (¼ inch) diameter, then press one side to form a teardrop.

- One strip, 3 mm (⅛ inch) by 5 cm (2 inches). Form into a tight coil.

MOUNTING

First, position all the pieces on the card without glue. For the petals, position the teardrops in the upper left-hand corner, with their points towards the centre. Attach the tight coil where the petal points meet.

Position three of the S scrolls along the short side of the card. Position the remaining five S scrolls along the top edge of the card. When you are happy with the layout, glue the pieces down, one at a time.

THREE-PETAL FLOWER WITH SCROLLS

CORNER SCROLL

Paper 80 gsm, 3 mm (⅛ inch) wide

Colour One or more colours

Quilling shapes S scroll, tight coil

Construction

Cut:

- Two strips, each 3 mm (⅛ inch) by 10 cm (4 inches). Form each strip into an S scroll 2 cm (¾ inch) long.
- Two strips, each 3 mm (⅛ inch) by 6 cm (2 ⁵⁄₁₆ inch). Form each strip into an S scroll 1 cm (⁷⁄₁₆ inch) long.
- Four strips, each 3 mm (⅛ inch) by 6 cm (2 ⁵⁄₁₆ inches). Form each strip into a tight coil.
- Four strips, each 3 mm (⅛ inch) by 5 cm (2 inches). Form each strip into a tight coil.
- Four strips, each 3 mm (⅛ inch) by 4 cm (1 ½ inches). Form each strip into a tight coil.
- Four strips, each 3 mm (⅛ inch) by 3 cm (1 ¼ inches). Form each strip into a tight coil.
- Four strips, each 3 mm (⅛ inch) by 2 cm (¾ inch). Form each strip into a tight coil.
- Four strips, each 3 mm (⅛ inch) by 1 cm (⁷⁄₁₆ inch). Form each strip into a tight coil.

MOUNTING

First, arrange all the pieces on the card without glue. Position the two 1 cm (⁷⁄₁₆ inch) S scrolls to form a heart at the top left-hand corner of the card. Next, position the 2 cm (¾ inch) S scrolls, one on the side edge, the other along the top edge. Position the remaining tight coils in descending order of size around the coiled ends of each of the large scrolls, as shown in the photograph. When you are happy with the layout, glue the pieces down, one at a time.

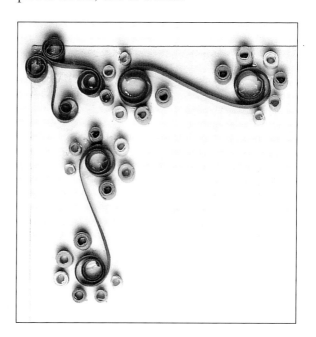

SIMPLE SNOWFLAKE

Paper 80 gsm, 3 mm (⅛ inch) wide

Colour One or more colours

Quilling shapes Tight coil, loose coil, teardrop

Construction

Cut:

- One strip, 3 mm (⅛ inch) by 20 cm (8 inches). Form into a tight coil.
- Five strips, each 3 mm (⅛ inch) by 8 cm (3 ⅛ inches). Form each strip into a tight coil.
- Five strips, each 3 mm (⅛ inch) by 10 cm (4 inches). Form each strip into a loose coil of 6 mm (¼ inch) diameter.
- Five strips, each 3 mm (⅛ inch) by 10 cm (4 inches). Form each strip into a loose coil of 6 mm (¼ inch) diameter, then press one side to form a teardrop.

MOUNTING

First, arrange all the pieces on the card without glue. Position the largest tight coil 2 cm (¾ inch) in from the side edge of the card and 2.5 cm (1 inch) down from the top. Now evenly space the five smaller tight coils around the largest tight coil. Fit the loose coils between the tight coils and then position the teardrops, with the pointed ends facing out, between the loose coils. When you are happy with the layout, glue the pieces down, one at a time.

SNOWFLAKE

Paper 80 gsm, 3 mm (⅛ inch) wide

Colour One or more colours

Quilling shapes Tight coil, loose coil, teardrop, eye, C scroll

Construction

Cut:

- One strip, 3 mm (⅛ inch) by 20 cm (8 inches). Form into a tight coil.
- Four strips, each 3 mm (⅛ inch) by 8 cm (3 ⅛ inches). Form each strip into a loose coil 6 mm (¼ inch) in diameter, then press one side to form a teardrop.
- Four strips, each 3 mm (⅛ inch) by 8 cm (3 ⅛ inches). Form each strip into a loose coil 6 mm (¼ inch) in diameter, then press both ends to form an eye.
- Eight strips, each 3 mm (⅛ inch) by 5 cm (2 inches). Form each strip into a loose coil 3 mm (⅛ inch) in diameter.
- Eight strips, each 3 mm (⅛ inch) by 6 cm (2 ⁵⁄₁₆ inches). Form each strip into a C scroll by coiling each end on the same side, leaving a 6 mm (¼ inch) straight section in the centre.

Mounting

First, arrange all the pieces on the card without glue. Position the 20 cm (8 inch) tight coil 2.5cm (1 inch) in from the side and top of the card. Now position the teardrops, with their points facing out, evenly around the centre coil.

Fit the eyes between the teardrops against the centre coil. Next, position the loose coils in the spaces between the tips of the teardrops and eyes. Then position the C scrolls so that they touch the edges of the loose coils and bridge the gap over the teardrops and eyes. When you are happy with the layout, glue the pieces down, one at a time.

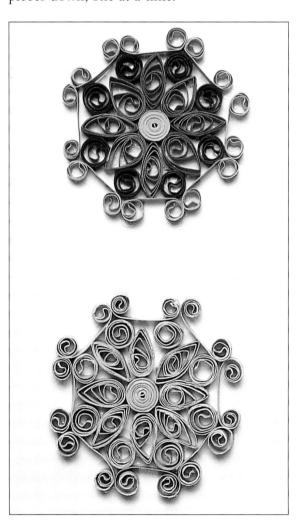

DRAGONFLY

Paper 80 gsm, 3 mm (⅛ inch) wide

Colour Two colours: one for the head, neck and body; one for the wings

Quilling shapes Tight coil, cone, eye

Construction

NOTE: This pattern uses tight coils mounted on their side.

Cut:

- One strip, 6 mm by 9 cm (3 ½ inches). Form into a tight coil. This piece will form the neck.
- 1 strip, 3 mm (⅛ inch) by 6 cm (2 ⁵⁄₁₆ inches). Form into a tight coil. This piece will form the head.
- 7 strips, each 3 mm (⅛ inch) by 3 cm (1 ¼ inches). Form each strip into a tight coil. These pieces will form the body.
- 1 strip, 3 mm (⅛ inch) by 5 cm (2 inches). Form into a tight coil then into a cone. This piece will form the tail. To make a cone, start it as a tight coil for three turns; then slowly move the feeding-in paper down slightly as you coil the rest of the way. This should make a tapered end for the dragonfly tail. Glue the end. You may have already accidentally made a cone when trying to do tight coils.
- Four strips, each 3 mm (⅛ inch) by 20 cm (8 inches). Form each strip into a 1 cm (⁷⁄₁₆ inch) loose coil then press each side to make an eye.

MOUNTING

First, arrange all the pieces on the card without glue. When you are happy with the layout, glue the pieces down, one at a time. All the body pieces are glued to each other on the end that touches the next piece as well as underneath (usually where the glue join is). Start with the neck first, then add the head.

Next, glue down the body pieces; these can be kept in a straight line or curved slightly. Now add the tail section. Add the wings with the narrowest end of the eye against the sides of the neck section and at a slight angle. If you wish, you can mark eyes on the head using a pen. When you are happy with your layout, glue the pieces down, one at a time.

HEATH BELLS

Paper 80 gsm, 3 mm (⅛ inch) wide

Colour Two colours: one for the bells, one for the stem and leaves

Quilling shapes Eye, cone

Construction

For the bells, cut eight strips, each 3 mm (⅛ inch) by 15 cm (6 inches). Form each strip into a cone 1 cm (⁷⁄₁₆ inch) long.

To make a cone, start to coil as for the tail of the Dragonfly on page 36, but keep turning slowly with the paper feeding in at a very slight angle. Don't worry if it doesn't work the first few times. Just undo the piece and try again. If you begin to get disheartened, try this simple method:

TIP

Make a tight coil and glue the end. Find a blunt pencil or biro and very gently push the centre of the coil until it forms a cone the right size over the end of the pencil or pen. If you push too hard and ruin it, don't worry. It's only a little bit of paper. Cut a new piece of paper and try again. Most quillers have had trouble with cones, even me. You will get the hang of it eventually.

For the large leaves, cut three strips, each 3 mm (⅛ inch) by 10 cm (4 inches). Form each strip into a loose coil of 1 cm (⁷⁄₁₆ inch) diameter, then press each end to form an eye.

For the small leaves, cut six strips, each 3 mm (⅛ inch) by 5 cm (2 inches). Form each strip into a loose coil of 6 mm (¼ inch) diameter, then press each side to form an eye.

For the stem, cut one strip, 3 mm (⅛ inch) by 4 cm (1 ½ inch). Curve the strip slightly.

Mounting

First, arrange all the pieces on the card without glue. Position the stem on its edge to the left-hand side of the card. Position the bells on either side of the stem, leaving enough space to fit the small leaves between them. Position the three larger leaves at the base of the stem. When you are happy with your layout, glue the pieces down, one at a time.

FAIRY SKIRTS

Paper 80 gsm, 3 mm (⅛ inch), 6 mm (⅛ inch) wide
and 8 mm (¼ inch) wide

Colour Four colours: three pale colours for the skirts, one colour for
the leaves and vine

Quilling shapes Dome (upside-down cup), fringing, cone

Construction

For the skirts, cut:

- Eight strips, each 3 mm (⅛ inch) by
  10 cm (4 inches)
- Eight strips, each 6 mm by 2 cm
  (¾ inch), finely fringed to within 2 mm
  (⅟₁₆ inch) of the edge.

Use a tiny bulldog clip to keep your fringing straight and to stop you cutting right through the strip. The clip is useful when cutting two or three strips at a time.

Join one end of the straight strip to one end of the fringed strip (they will look like a toothbrush). Form into a tight coil from the unfringed end to form a dome shape. The dome shape is simply a cup shape turned upside down. The fringing should hang down around the open end of the dome. If you have trouble, use the 'tight coil push system'

(as described in Heath Bells on page 37) using an object with a round end such as a biro or pen.

For the stems, cut eight strips, each 3 mm (⅛ inch) by 2 cm (¾ inch). Coil each strip to form a small cone 6 mm (¼ inch) long.

For the vine, cut one strip, (⅛ inch) by 10 cm (4 inches). Fold the strip into a zigzag of eight folds.

Mounting

First, arrange all the pieces on the card without glue. Attach each stem to the top of a dome, then allow to dry. Position the vine strip along the top edge of the card. Allow to dry, then add the fairy skirts, positioning the cone end into the upward-pointing spaces of the zigzag. When you are happy with the layout, glue the pieces down, one at a time.

WATTLE SPRAY

Paper 80 gsm, 3 mm (⅛ inch) and 6 mm (¼ inch) wide

Colour Two colours: one for the blossoms, one for the leaves and stem

Quilling shapes Fringed tight coil (the finer the fringing, the fluffier the finished blossom), leaf

Construction

For the blossoms, cut long strips of paper 6 mm (¼ inch) and finely fringe to a depth of 3 mm (⅛ inch). Use a tiny bulldog clip as your depth gauge. When complete, tear the longer strips into nine shorter strips, each 7 cm (2 ¾ inches) long. Form each short strip into a tight coil. When the glue is dry, spread the fringing out and down to cover the uncut section, like a little umbrella.

For the stem, cut one strip, 3 mm (⅛ inch) by 7 cm (2 ¾ inches). Curve this strip slightly.

The leaves are made in three sizes. To make a leaf shape, first make an eye shape of the specified size, then bend the ends in opposite directions to form a Z or S shape.

For the large leaves, cut two strips, each 3 mm (⅛ inch) by 12 cm (¾ inch). Form each strip into a loose coil to a diameter of 1 cm (⁷⁄₁₆ inch), then press into a leaf shape as described above.

For the medium leaves, cut eight strips, each 3 mm (⅛ inch) by 8 cm (3 ⅛ inches). Form each strip into a loose coil 7 mm (½ inch) in diameter, then press into a leaf shape as described above.

For the small leaves, cut two strips, each 3 mm (⅛ inch) by 5 cm (2 inches.) Form each strip into a loose coil 6 mm (¼ inch) in diameter, then press into a leaf shape as described above.

Mounting

First, position all the pieces on the card without glue. Curve the stem strip and position it from the left-hand bottom corner to the centre top edge. Position blossoms alternately and evenly along the sides of the stem. Be sure to allow the fringing to go over the stem. Most of the stem will be covered by fringing. Leave spaces for the leaves. Place the two small leaves at the tip of the stem and the two large leaves at the base. Place the medium leaves along the stem and between the blossoms, alternating the sides on which they are placed. When you are happy with the layout, glue the pieces down, one at a time.

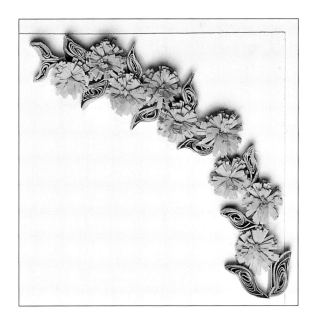

SMILEY

Paper 80 gsm, 3 mm (¼ inch) and 6 mm (⅛ inch) wide

Colour Four colours: one for the hair, one for the centres of the eyes, one for the eyes and mouth, one for the nose, lips and cheeks

Quilling shapes Fringed tight coil, dome, crescent (using two colours), eye (using two colours), loose coil

Construction

For the hair, cut six strips, each 6 mm (¼ inch) by 6 cm (2 ⁵⁄₁₆ inches). Fringe each strip to a depth of 4 mm (⁵⁄₁₆ inch), then form into a tight coil.

For the nose, cut one strip, 3 mm (⅛ inch) by 20 cm (8 inches). Form into a tight coil then into a dome.

For the eyes, cut two strips, 3 mm (⅛ inch) by 3 cm (1 ¼ inches). These will form the eye centres. Cut two strips, 3 mm (⅛ inch) by 7 cm (2 ¾ inch). Join one end of each of these strips to one end of an eye-centre colour strip to form a strip 10 cm (4 inches) long. Starting from the eye-centre colour, form the strip into a loose coil, then into an eye shape.

For the cheeks, cut two strips, each 3 mm (⅛ inch) by (1 ¼ inches) and form into a loose coil of 3 mm (⅛ inch) diameter.

For the mouth, cut one strip, 3 mm (⅛ inch) by 20 cm (8 inches). This piece will form the lips. Cut another strip, 3 mm (⅛ inch) by 20 cm (8 inches) from another colour. Join these two strips to form a 40 cm (16 inch) strip and coil, starting from the lip-colour end, to form a loose coil of 1.5 cm (⅝ inch) diameter, then press into a crescent shape.

MOUNTING

First, arrange all the pieces on the card without glue. When you are pleased with the layout, glue the pieces down, one at a time.

DAISY CHAIN

Paper 80 gsm, 3 mm (⅛ inch) and 6 mm (¼ inch) wide.

Colour Four colours: two for the petals, one for the centres, one for the leaves

Quilling shapes Tight coil with fringing (using two colours), teardrop

Construction

First, construct the blossom pieces.

For the petals, from the first colour, cut three strips, each 6 mm (¼ inch) by 8 cm (3 ⅛ inch). Finely fringe to a depth of 4 mm (⁵⁄₁₆ inch).

From the second petal colour, cut three strips, each 6 mm (¼ inch) by 8 cm (3 ⅛ inches). Finely fringe to a depth of 4 mm (⁵⁄₁₆ inch).

For the centre, cut six strips, each 3 mm (⅛ inch) by 5 cm (2 inches).

Join one straight strip to the uncut section of each of the fringing strips. Each strip should look like a toothbrush. Form each strip into a tight coil from the straight end. When the glue is dry, spread the fringing to expose the centre. This forms a daisy.

For the leaves, cut twelve strips, each 3 mm (⅛ inch) by 6 cm (2 ⁵⁄₁₆ inch). Form each strip into a loose coil 6 mm (¼ inch) in diameter then press on both sides to form a teardrop.

MOUNTING

First, arrange the pieces on the card without glue. Position three blossoms evenly down the left-hand side and three across the top. Position leaves with their points towards the blossom, two leaves per blossom. Position the corner leaves at right angles. When you are happy with the layout, glue the pieces down, one at a time.

Daisy chain

CHILDREN'S GALLERY

These patterns were tested by a number of eager children. Samples of their best pieces follow.

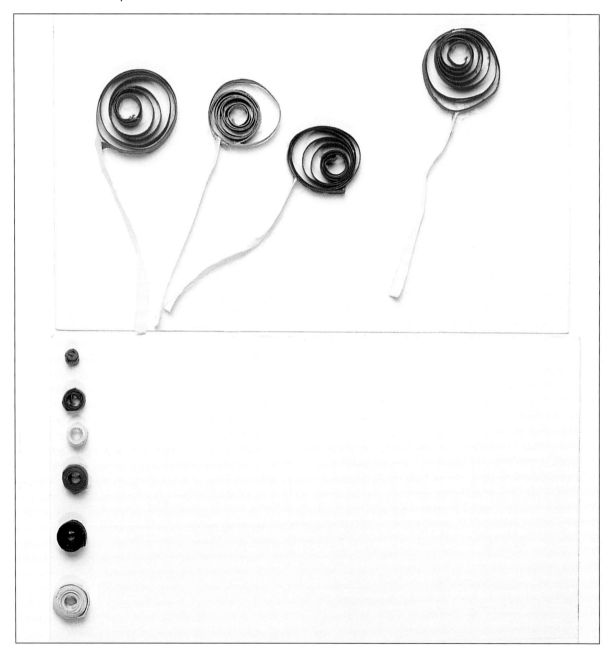

JACOB, AGED 12

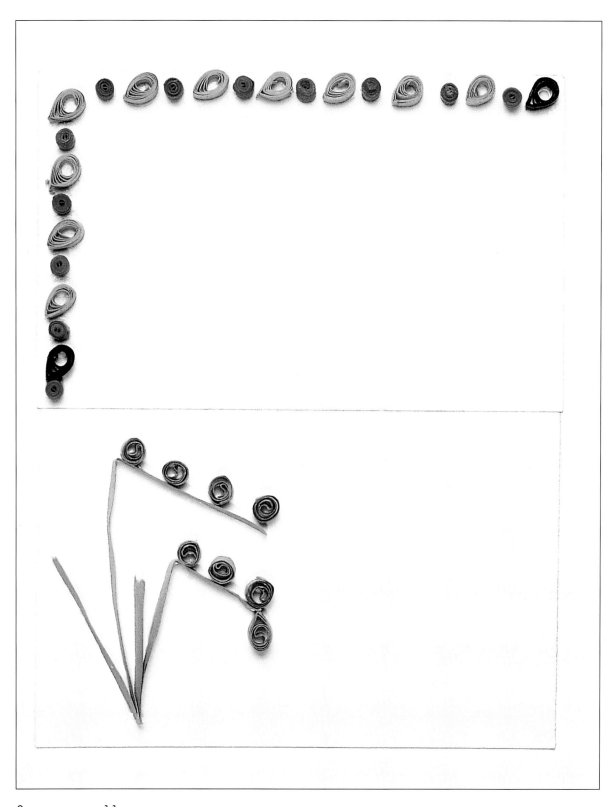

SHARAI, AGED 11

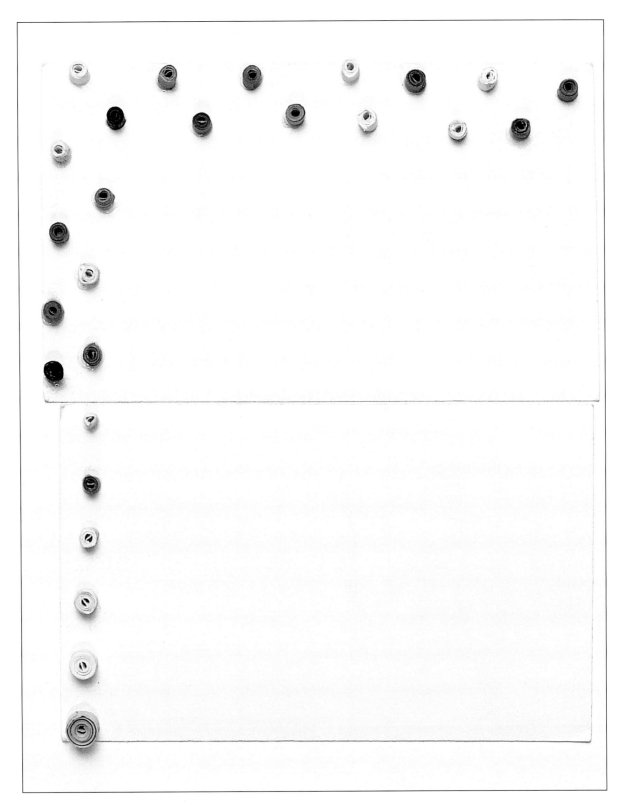

Martiiqua, aged 10

SHARMONEE, AGED 10

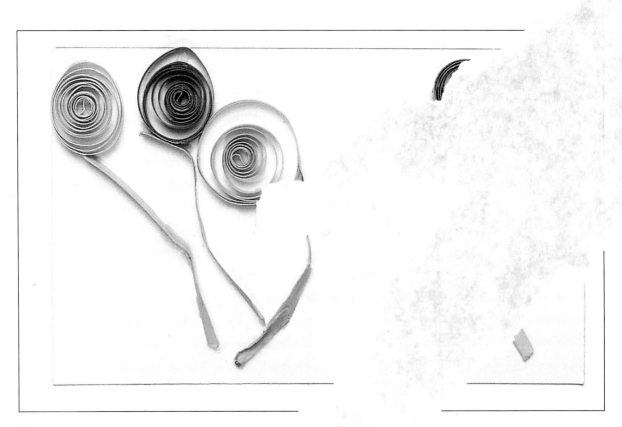

Travis, aged 6